Hope & Wonder

ADVENT DEVOTIONAL FOR FAMILIES

ANNA TURNER

SCAN ME
Download the Extras

TABLE OF CONTENTS

Note to Parents

Thank you for making Jesus the focus of your family's Christmas. You are giving your kids an extraordinary gift by teaching them about Him. This devotional will bring your family together during Advent to focus on Jesus and scripture while learning more together.

Society tries to convince us that Christmas must be "magical" for our children, and good parents buy all the wishes on their list. This magic brings a stranger into their home with all the gifts, but what of the Truth of Christmas? Where does Jesus fit into this magical, self-centered approach to Christmas?

Our enemy would love nothing more than for our children to believe Christmas is all about them, so they miss the greatest gift this world has ever received. As parents, we are responsible for guiding and teaching our children. Christmas allows us to introduce the Gospel, celebrate our Savior, and begin planting the Truth of this gift in our children's hearts.

When I had my first child, many thoughts ran through my mind about Christmas. I was fully prepared to bring all the "magic" money could buy to our Christmases. As I was planning her first Christmas, I realized none of my plans included the birth of Jesus. Yikes! This realization led me to research more about Christmas traditions that focus on Jesus and ultimately to check my heart about what was most important to me about the season. Through that research, I stumbled upon the tradition of Advent.

I never understood Advent growing up. I thought it was just about the little chocolates that come out of the paper windows as you countdown to Santa coming. So, I was pleasantly surprised to find out about the depth and long-standing traditions of Advent. I wanted something more for my family as we celebrated our Savior's birth, and the Advent tradition is a beautiful way to remember. It's not bound to certain sects of Christianity; we can all participate in this joyous tradition.

As we light the candles during Advent, I see the wonder in my children's eyes as the flames flicker and the shadows dance around the room. They don't realize it, but they are spending weeks learning and memorizing scriptures about the wonderful hope we have in Jesus. They may be small, but not a moment is wasted when you invest in your children by teaching them the Truth- through Jesus, we have hope and wonder.

Understanding Advent

Advent, in some form, has been celebrated for centuries. As with many traditions, Advent has transformed over the years and now includes candles and an Advent wreath.

The word *Advent* comes from the Latin word *adventus*. In Latin, *adventus* has several meanings, including arriving or coming. Interestingly, in ancient Rome, two definitions of *adventus* were celebrating a victory on the battlefield and a royal leader's birthday. What a perfect word to commemorate our Savior as we celebrate His birthdate and His victorious second coming.[1]

Advent focuses on four main themes: hope, peace, joy, and love. Each of these themes points to truths found in scripture about the birth of Jesus and the promises of God for us. These themes also challenge us to take the Gospel beyond our homes and share it with others.

As you begin the devotional, let this be a springboard for more study and discussion. Throughout the book, you will not find printed scripture. I did this intentionally to challenge children to look up the scriptures themselves in a printed Bible. Use this time to reinforce looking up scripture and teaching them how the Bible is organized.

The hymn studies help your family learn more about these theologically rich Christmas anthems. They are old and have some tricky words, so these are perfect to study together and discuss the more profound meaning. Learning about hymns will encourage kids to sing with more conviction once they understand the significance of those words.

The family challenges will help bring your family together for a common goal. Encourage your children to develop the idea; they will be more likely to buy into the challenge. Serving the Lord together can strengthen a family bond and help children learn more about service.

Check the Notes at the back of this book for more resources and lists. There is a list of family challenge ideas if you are stuck. Remember your download for additional activity pages, memory verses, and more. The QR code is on the contents page for your free download.

You can use this Advent devotional weekly as designed or structure it however is best for your family. Schedule a time to come together to complete it. Whether it's daily or once weekly, any time is better than no time. Discipling our children is critical, so make time for it. Their knowing about Jesus is of eternal importance.

Lighting the Advent Wreath

This devotional does not require you to use an Advent wreath, but if your family would like to, here's more information about the wreath and lighting the candles. Advent starts four Sundays before Christmas Day, so the date changes yearly.

There is so much symbolism surrounding Advent and the elements used to celebrate it. With the Advent wreath, you first will notice the round shape in which you arrange the candles. The never-ending circle symbolizes God, with no beginning or end, Jesus' unending love for us, and our eternal life through salvation. You can add ever-greens to your wreath, symbolizing eternal life as well.[2]

The candles have traditional colors that vary depending on the user, but most have three purple candles, one pink and one white. The purple colors are traditionally for royalty. Pink is for joy, and the white candle symbolizes the purity and sinlessness of Jesus.

As you light the candles in sequence each week, they remind us of the light Jesus brought to the world and the darkness He destroyed. Each week, you burn an additional candle, and the light grows brighter, reminding us that sharing the Gospel impacts the Kingdom of God by making disciples.

Here's what the Advent wreath tradition looks like for our family. Each Sunday, we light a new candle. Throughout the week, we continue lighting the candles for that week at dinner. We read through scripture and discuss the theme of the candle. (Find the themes on the next page.) Since we have small children, we try to help them learn one memory verse weekly.

Advent Wreath
MONTH OUTLOOK

WEEK 1
Purple Candle of Hope
Light One Purple Candle

The *Prophecy Candle* reminds us of the prophecies and promises of the coming Savior.

WEEK 2
Purple Candle of Love
Light Two Purple Candles

The *Bethlehem Candle* reminds us of the place where Jesus was born, thus fulfilling the prophecy.

WEEK 3
Pink Candle of Joy
Light Two Purple and One Pink Candle

The *Shepherd's Candle* reminds us to rejoice.

WEEK 4
Purple Candle of Peace
Light Three Purple and One Pink Candle

The *Angel's Candle* reminds us of their shared good news and the peace Jesus brings.

CHRISTMAS DAY
White Candle of Christ | Light all of the Candles
The *Christ Candle* reminds us of Jesus' sinlessness and His ultimate victory over sin.

Week One

Hope

Our hope is different than the world's hope. The world's hope is wishful, but our hope is in Jesus. He came to earth as a baby, willingly died for our sins, rose from the dead, and is coming again.

You may have hoped for a new gift or a win for your favorite team. You couldn't be sure those things would happen, but you wished they would. The hope Jesus provides is not fleeting; our hope is infallible because it is truth based on God's holy Word.

God promised He would send a savior to the human race, and He did. Jesus promised He would come again, and He will. Our hope is in a God who cannot lie or break His promises. The Bible is full of proof of His faithfulness.

This week, you will read prophecies in the Old Testament that prove Jesus is our Messiah.

Write Isaiah 9:6 in the space below, and spend the week memorizing this scripture.

_____

_____

_____

_____

_____

_____

☐ Genesis 3:15   ☐ Micah 5:2

☐ Isaiah 7:14   ☐ 2 Samuel 7:12-13

☐ Isaiah 9:6-7   ☐ John 8:12

Read Genesis 3:15, then look up and define the word "protevangelium."

_____

_____

How is this promise fulfilled?

_____

_____

_____

_____

List the names of the Son the prophet mentioned.

_____

_____

_____

_____

_____

_____

_____

_____

_____

_____

_____

Fill in the blank. Jesus said, "I am the _____ of the world."

This week's family challenge is all about hope. There are so many around us who feel hopeless. As Christians we know the remedy for the hopelessness, but others may not. So, it's time to share! How can you or your family share hope with those around you this week? Use the space provided below to write notes about what hope means, and ideas for your family challenge. Remember our hope is in Jesus, and He will never fail us.

See page 75 for family challenge ideas.

Family Journal

Come, Thou Long Expected Jesus

by Charles Wesley

Come, Thou long expected Jesus
Born to set Thy people free;
From our fears and sins release us,
Let us find our rest in Thee.
Israel's strength and consolation,
Hope of all the earth Thou art;
Dear desire of every nation,
Joy of every longing heart.

Born Thy people to deliver,
Born a child and yet a King,
Born to reign in us forever,
Now Thy gracious kingdom bring.
By Thine own eternal Spirit
Rule in all our hearts alone;
By Thine all sufficient merit,
Raise us to Thy glorious throne.

By Thine all sufficient merit,
Raise us to Thy glorious throne.

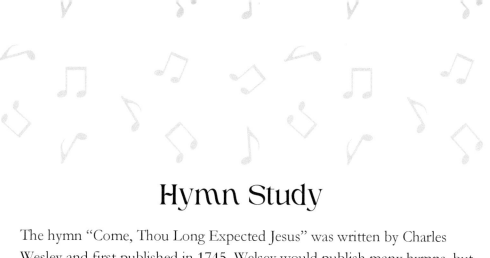

Hymn Study

The hymn "Come, Thou Long Expected Jesus" was written by Charles Wesley and first published in 1745. Welsey would publish many hymns, but this is one of his most lasting.[3]

This song is great for Advent as it focuses on our hope in Jesus and looks toward the future of His coming again. It is truly an anthem based on scripture.

First, read through the hymn together. When you come to unfamiliar words, circle them. Take turns discussing what you think the hymn means. How does this hymn point to Jesus?

Look up the definitions of a few circled words and write them below.

_____

_____

_____

_____

_____

_____

_____

_____

_____

_____

Spend time listening to the hymn this week. Pick out your family's favorite part of the hymn and write it below.

Old Testament Prophecy	New Testament Fulfillment
Isaiah 7:14	Matthew 2:5-6
Micah 5:2	Luke 2:6-7
Isaiah 9:6	Matthew 1:23

Match the Old Testament prophecies to the fulfillments found in the New Testament. Turn it into a race and see who can find the scripture reference in the Bible first!

DID YOU KNOW?
The Messiah had to be of a certain genealogy. The biblical requirements said he would be descended from Abraham, the tribe of Judah, and the line of David. Jesus met all of these.

Week
Two

Love

God's love is our greatest example of love. It is hard to imagine God loving us so much that He would send His only son to die for our sins, but He did. Jesus came willingly and gave His life for us. Without knowing the perfect love of God, we cannot truly love others.

Love is more than an emotion or a quick word spoken from habit, and you may have been betrayed or hurt by someone who said they love you. In our minds we equate God's love with the love we receive from someone else, but there's no comparison. All humans, even those who love us, are imperfect and will disappoint and sometimes hurt our feelings. God will not. His love is perfect.

This week's scripture reading will teach you what we should do in response to His love.

Write 1 John 4:10 in the space below, and spend the week memorizing this scripture.

☐ Micah 5:2   ☐ Luke 2:4-6

☐ Matthew 2:5-6   ☐ John 7:42

☐ Luke 1:26-38   ☐ 1 John 4:10-11

Where was Jesus born?

_____

_____

Answer this question with scripture, "What is impossible with God?"

_____

_____

_____

_____

After reading 1 John 4:10, what did God do to show His love for us, and then how should we treat others?

_____

_____

_____

_____

_____

_____

_____

_____

_____

_____

_____

_____

_____

_____

_____

_____

Has someone ever shown you love through an act of kindness? This week's family challenge focuses on showing others God's love through acts of kindness. Scripture tells us we are to be known by our love. Find a way to show someone kindness this week. Start by reading Matthew 22:37-39. Use the space below for notes and challenge ideas.

See page 75 for family challenge ideas.

Family Journal

DID YOU KNOW?

King David was also born in Bethlehem. Jesus is a descendant of David as we learn in Isaiah 9:6-7.

O Little Town of Bethlehem

by Phillips Brooks

O little town of Bethlehem
How still we see thee lie
Above thy deep and dreamless sleep
The silent stars go by
Yet in thy dark streets shineth
The everlasting light
The hopes and fears of all the years
Are met in thee tonight

For Christ is born of Mary
And gathered all above
While mortals sleep, the angels keep
Their watch of wondering love

O morning stars together
Proclaim thy holy birth
And praises sing to God the King
And peace to men on earth

Hymn Study

Phillips Brooks wrote "O Little Town of Bethlehem" in 1868. After the Civil War ended, Brooks spent a year traveling through Europe and visiting the Holy Land. It was his time spent in Bethlehem that would later inspire his poem.

Brooks wrote the poem several years after his time in the Holy Land to share with his Sunday School class. The church organist set the poem to music, and it was performed at the Church of the Holy Trinity in Philadelphia for the first time.[5]

Read through the hymn together. When you come to unfamiliar words, circle them. Take turns discussing what you think the hymn means. How does this hymn point the listener to Jesus?

Look up the definitions of a few circled words and write them below.

_____

_____

_____

_____

_____

_____

_____

_____

_____

_____

_____

_____

Spend time listening to the hymn this week. Pick out your family's favorite part of the hymn and write it below.

Using 1 John 4:10-11 as inspiration, create scripture art using words, pictures, or both.

Week Three

Joy

Joy comes from knowing Christ as your Savior. We can have this joy because our Savior Jesus brought us back to our heavenly Father through His sacrifice on the cross.

Have you ever been really happy about a gift, but it broke? Your happiness was gone and replaced with disappointment. The happy feeling didn't last. Joy is different.

How can we be joy-filled no matter the situation around us? Because God gives joy, and no one can take it from you. Even though hard things will happen in your life, you can be joyful knowing God is on your side.

As you read the scriptures this week, notice the joy the shepherds experienced at the news of the Savior's birth.

Write 1 Peter 1:8 in the space below, and spend the week memorizing this scripture.

☐ Psalm 71:23   ☐ John 16:22

☐ Luke 1:47   ☐ Romans 5:11

☐ Luke 2:8-20   ☐ 1 Peter 1:8

What was the good news shared with the shepherds?

_____

_____

_____

_____

_____

_____

_____

What did they do after hearing this news? Would you have done the same, why or why not?

_____

_____

_____

_____

_____

_____

_____

_____

_____

_____

_____

_____

_____

_____

How can believing in something you can't see bring you so much joy that it's impossible to describe? (See 1 Peter 1:8)

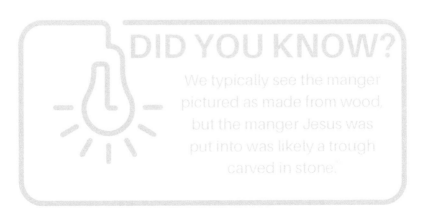

DID YOU KNOW?

We typically see the manger pictured as made from wood, but the manger Jesus was put into was likely a trough carved in stone.

It's time to rejoice! As believers we have joy that unbelievers do not understand. Has anyone ever asked you how you could be smiling and content while going through something difficult? We know it's because our joy is in Jesus, and we know the promises of God are true. This week's challenge is to show and tell someone about the joy of the Lord in your life. Use the space below for family testimonies of joy and challenge ideas.

See page 75 for family challenge ideas.

Family Journal

Joy to the World

by Isaac Watts

Joy to the world, the Lord is come!
Let earth receive her King!
Let every heart prepare Him room,
and heav'n and nature sing,
and heav'n and nature sing,
and heav'n, and heav'n and nature sing.

Joy to the earth, the Savior reigns!
Let men their songs employ,
while fields and floods, rocks, hills, and plains
repeat the sounding joy,
repeat the sounding joy,
repeat, repeat the sounding joy.

No more let sins and sorrows grow,
nor thorns infest the ground;
He comes to make His blessings flow
far as the curse is found,
far as the curse is found,
far as, far as the curse is found.

He rules the world with truth and grace,
and makes the nations prove
the glories of His righteousness
and wonders of His love,
and wonders of His love,
and wonders, wonders of His love.

Hymn Study

The hymn "Joy to the World" was written by Isaac Watts and published in the early 1700s. Watts believed that singing and worship should be done in our own words, so he spent years working to bring new hymns to the world. "Joy to the World" was written from his understanding of Psalm 98.[7]

First, read through the hymn together. Then, look up Psalm 98. Note any similarities in words and phrases in "Joy to the World" and Psalm 98. Use the space below for notes.

Notice this significant difference between the two. Psalm 98 is before Jesus' birth. "Joy to the World" is Watts' praise of the prophesied Messiah fulfilled through the birth of Jesus.

Spend time listening to the hymn this week. Pick out your family's favorite part of the hymn and write it below.

Create a comic strip about Luke 2:8-20.

Week
Four

Peace

Jesus is our peace. He brought peace to us through salvation by restoring us back to God through his sacrifice on the cross. His first coming brought peace to our souls; His second coming will bring peace to the earth.

You will have situations in your life that are stressful, scary, or uncontrollable; how can you have peace in those situations? Peace of God does not mean there will never be conflict in your life. It does mean that no matter what you face, your soul is at peace with God through Jesus, and you can have the peace of God knowing He will never leave you.

Throughout this week's reading, you will discover more about our peace with God and how we need to let His peace rule in our hearts. Thanksgiving (not the holiday) plays a role in peace as well.

Write Luke 2:14 in the space below, and spend the week memorizing this scripture.

☐ Luke 2:14   ☐ Romans 5:1
☐ John 3:16-17 ☐ Colossians 1:20
☐ John 16:33   ☐ Colossians 3:15

What does the coming of Jesus bring to the world, and how does it relate to peace?

_____

_____

_____

_____

_____

_____

_____

_____

_____

What does it mean to let the "peace of God" rule in your heart, and why is it important to be thankful to God? (See Colossians 3:15)

_____

_____

_____

_____

_____

_____

_____

_____

_____

_____

_____

_____

How does the peace of God differ from peace in the world?

The final week of this Advent journey focuses on peace, which is sometimes the opposite of what is taking place around us the last week before Christmas. Many people are feeling pressure and anxiety, among other things, as we get closer to Christmas Day. This week's family challenge is to find a way to share peace, the Gospel, with others. Start by reading Ephesians 2:14-22. Use the space below for notes and family challenge ideas.

See page 75 for family challenge ideas.

Family Journal

O Holy Night

by Placide Cappeau

O holy night, the stars are brightly shining;
It is the night of the dear Savior's birth!
Long lay the world in sin and error pining,
Till He appeared and the soul felt its worth.
A thrill of hope, the weary soul rejoices,
For yonder breaks a new and glorious morn.
Fall on your knees, O hear the angel voices!
O night divine, O night when Christ was born!
O night, O holy night, O night divine!

Led by the light of a faith serenely beaming,
With glowing hearts by His cradle we stand.
So led by light of a star so sweetly gleaming,
Here came the wise men from Orient land.
The King of kings lay thus in lowly manger,
In all our trials born to be our friend!
He knows our need—to our weakness is no stranger.
Behold your king; before Him lowly bend!
Behold your king; before Him lowly bend!

Truly He taught us to love one another;
His law is love and His Gospel is peace.
Chains shall He break, for the slave is our brother
And in His name all oppression shall cease.
Sweet hymns of joy in grateful chorus raise we,
Let all within us praise His holy name!
Christ is the Lord! O praise His name forever!
His pow'r and glory evermore proclaim!
His pow'r and glory evermore proclaim!

Hymn Study

The hymn "O Holy Night" was written by Placide Cappeau in France. Cappeau was tasked to write a Christmas poem in 1847. He wrote the poem, *Cantique de Noël,* from his research of the book of Luke.

The poem was translated into English by John Dwight in 1855. Dwight found the third verse to be of great significance, considering slavery during that time in history.

In 1906, "O Holy Night" was the first Christmas song broadcast on the radio. Reginald Fessenden broadcast live on the radio, read scripture from the book of Luke, then played "O Holy Night" on his violin, singing the last verse.[8]

First, read through the hymn together. Take turns discussing what you think the hymn means. Rewrite one verse in your own words. Use the space provided.

Spend time listening to the hymn this week. Pick out your family's favorite part of the hymn and write it below.

_____

_____

_____

_____

_____

_____

_____

_____

_____

_____

_____

_____

_____

_____

_____

_____

_____

_____

_____

_____

_____

_____

_____

_____

_____

_____

Unscramble these words then read Isaiah 9:6.

crniPe fo ecPae

_ _ _ _ _ _   _ _

_ _ _ _ _

DID YOU KNOW?

We do not know the number of magi, wise men, that visited Jesus. We typically show three wise men because we know there were three gifts given.

Christmas Day

Christmas

Christmas is here, but this is only the beginning! You have spent the last month learning about hope, love, joy, and peace. All of these come together in God's grand plan for our redemption through Jesus.

God's great love for us sent Jesus, our hope, to bring peace to our souls and inexplicable joy to our lives as we follow Him.

Your family has set out on challenges each week to share the Gospel with others as we have all been commanded to do. Let this month be the beginning of a great purpose-filled life lived for God.

Write Romans 10:9-10 in the space below, and spend time memorizing the scripture.

☐ Romans 6:23   ☐ Titus 2:11-14

☐ Romans 15:13   ☐ 1 Corinthians 15:57

What is the "free gift of God?"

_____

_____

_____

_____

_____

_____

First Corinthians 15:57 says we have victory over what?

_____

_____

_____

_____

_____

_____

_____

_____

_____

_____

_____

_____

_____

_____

Christmas is here! How will your family honor and celebrate Jesus' birth today? While you may have Christmas Day traditions already in place, today's family challenge is to make time to remember Jesus. In the space below write out the ideas for you family challenge.

See page 75 for family challenge ideas.

Add or draw a photo of your family. Write a Christmas memory below it.

CHRISTMAS MEMORIES

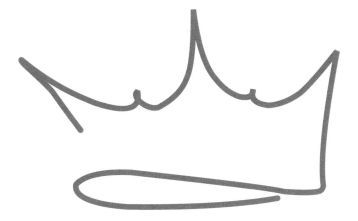

"Therefore, stay awake, for you do not know on what day your Lord is coming."

MATTHEW 24:42 ESV

Notes

Source Notes

1. Beale, Stephen. "The Deeper Meaning of Advent in Latin." Catholic Exchange. Last Modified December 1, 2021. https://catholicexchange.com/the-deeper-meaning-of-advent-in-latin/

2. Ryan, Joel. "What Is an Advent Wreath? Meaning and Purpose of Wreath and Candles." Christianity.com. Last Modified November 2, 2021. https://www.christianity.com/wiki/holidays/advent-wreath-meaning-of-advent-candles.html

3. Hymnary.org. "Charles Wesley." Accessed October 5, 2023. https://hymnary.org/text/come_thou_long_expected_jesus_born_to

4. Harbin, Michael A. *The Promise and the Blessing: A Historical Survey of the Old and New Testaments.* (Zondervan, Grand Rapids, MI. 2005).

5. Hymnary.org. "Phillips Brooks." Accessed October 5, 2023. https://hymnary.org/text/come_thou_long_expected_jesus_born_to

6. Harbin, 2005.

7. Poblete, Alyssa. "Joy to the World: A Christmas Hymn Reconsidered." The Gospel Coalition. Last Modified December 22, 2014.https://www.thegospelcoalition.org/article/joy-to-the-world-a-classic-christmas-hymn-reconsidered/

8. Christmascarols.us. Cantique de Noël. Accessed October 5, 2023. https://christmascarols.us/history/o_holy_night.aspx

9. Harbin, 2005.

Family Challenge Ideas

Week 1

- Pray for the hopeless
- Send a card to someone
- Witness of the Hope we have in Jesus

Week 2

- Show kindness to someone in your home
- Send a kind note
- Leave a snack for the mail carrier
- Help a friend

Week 3

- Send a care package to someone
- Share a smile
- Go caroling

Week 4

- Give away Bibles
- Practice sharing the Gospel
- Give away small gifts to remind people of Jesus, like a bracelet or toy

Christmas

- Have a birthday party for Jesus
- Make a cake
- Read Luke 2 as a family

Anna Turner

AUTHOR

Anna holds a Bachelor's degree in psychology and is a devoted mother of three. She is married to her best friend, Matt Turner. Anna's passion lies in helping parents discover creative and meaningful ways to teach their children about Jesus at home.

As the creator of Turner Littles, she is dedicated to equipping parents with valuable resources to encourage the spiritual growth of their little ones. Her work guides families to nurture a love for Christ in their homes.

Join her on her journey of helping parents make little disciples on social media @turnerlittles and online at TurnerLittles.com.

Made in the USA
Columbia, SC
25 November 2024

47096058R00044